Life In An American Homeless Shelter

2011

Danbury, Connecticut

Guy S. LaGrotta

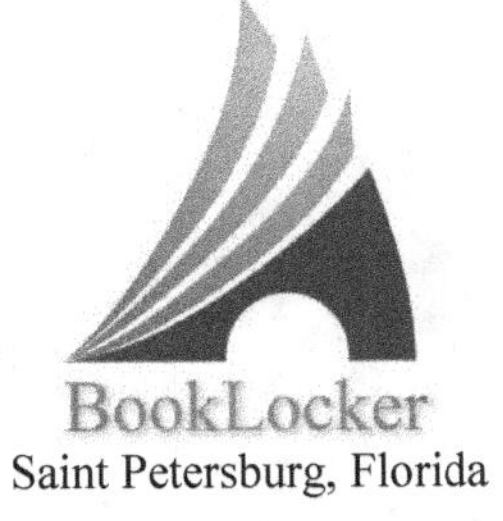

BookLocker

Saint Petersburg, Florida

TABLE OF CONTENTS

Introduction

Every dark cloud has a silver lining so they say. For me the silver lining of the current Coronavirus lockdown could be that I now have the time and inclination to write about an even worse period in my life back in 2011, when I found myself virtually penniless and had to seek refuge in a homeless shelter. Looking back to March 11th through July 25th of that year, I still find it hard to believe such a thing actually happened to me. The whole experience seems like a bad dream now-- not the short, intense nightmarish kind that scares the hell out of you, but a muted slow-motion one that would eventually last for more than four months. What kept me from giving up during this time was knowing deep in my heart, *I could do much better than this*-- that my homeless shelter stay was a temporary phase in my life, and as long as I didn't despair I would, with the kindly help of others to be sure, work my way out of the mess I had gotten myself into.

Another thing that helped to make the experience bearable was when I gradually learned to stop obsessing about my own predicament and start focusing more on what was happening around me, like a detached observer. Such detachment was not always easy to maintain (to say the least) but when I did so I soon became fascinated by what I saw. Of course not every day was memorable. Much of my shelter stay was forgettably boring, but there were a number of events that I remember vividly, and always will. They run the range from deeply troubling to merely annoying, and to finally-- in a few instances, downright comical.

A small portion of what I am about to describe is secondhand information from reliable sources. This is because I never tried to verify every bit of news on my own like an investigative reporter. In a homeless shelter the most closely-guarded item, I learned right away, was not money or a cell phone but personal information, and asking a nosy question at the wrong time could be risky.

My primary goal was to survive, so I was careful not to do anything that might unduly jeopardize my safety. The following account is as accurate as my memory allows; only the names of the people are fictitious and are mostly monikers, each of which I thought best captured the essence of a particular personality.

Part I

A Very Sad But Necessary Task
Choosing A Shelter
First Night & The Following Morning

The veterinarian's prognosis confirmed my worst fears and I felt a large lump forming in my throat. My little dog's heart disease had reached the stage where further treatment would be useless. As I stood there upset, cradling my dog in my arms, the vet excused himself from the exam room and left us alone for several minutes. When he returned I reluctantly agreed to his recommendation. Quietly he said, "I'll be back in a few minutes. You may hold Calvin in your arms if you like while I give him the injection. He shouldn't feel any pain-

- his heart will stop beating in less than a minute but his eyes might remain open." I nodded yes and began to scratch Calvin tenderly and let him lick my hands for the last few times. After what seemed like forever, the vet returned and everything went according to plan. As soon as the vet removed his stethoscope, looked at me and nodded, I took one last look into my little dog's open but now lifeless eyes-- and broke down in tears.

Later that night as I was reliving the day's events in my mind's eye, I felt heartbroken but relieved. I did what had to be done. Calvin had lived a good long life for a dog-- 17 years, and had reached the point where he could no longer get up by himself. At least his problems were over with. It was now Wednesday evening, March 9th, and I had to be out of my ex-landlady's house by Friday morning, March 11th, at the latest. I did have some meager savings left (which would be added to from time to time by concerned relatives) and I did have transportation in the form of a high-mileage, 13-year-old minivan. (The vet's bill for Calvin's last visit would take me well over a year to pay off).

Before I knew it, Friday morning arrived and off I went in search of a safe and secure place to spend the night. I had been told by a knowledgeable source that Danbury was the best place to look since it had, not only its own city-run homeless shelter, but at least two other privately-run ones as well. Danbury was also the closest large city to the small town where I had been living. By late afternoon I managed to find the city shelter at 41 New Street, but it was locked and nobody was there. In the meantime I would check out some of the other privately-run shelters nearby.

The Dorothy Day Shelter was the closest one, literally a stone's throw from 41 New Street. Located directly behind the Dorothy Day Soup Kitchen on Spring Street, the shelter entrance was at the rear of a small courtyard that was connected to the street by a narrow driveway. As soon as I turned the corner to walk up the driveway, I noticed someone locking the shelter's front door. Hurrying along, I hailed him and asked if I could have a quick look inside. He was a tall, older man, somewhat gruff, but he agreed and unlocked the door. As

I stepped over the threshold and began to make out the interior of a dimly lit, cramped-looking room, I was hit by an odor that brought to mind dirty laundry, sweaty locker room, and musty attic, all rolled into one pungent brew. I gasped and quickly stepped backwards. After taking a few deep breaths I thanked the man and hurried back to Spring Street. "Strike One," I said to myself.

There was still nobody around the city shelter, so I decided to look at the other privately-run shelter that I knew about which was located in the basement of the Congregational Church on West Street, a short drive away. As I pulled up I noticed a couple of cars with people in them parked outside. Here apparently was a good opportunity for me to find out about this place from those who may have stayed here before, and who seemed to be waiting for it to open. I approached the first car and gently tapped on the driver's window. It was starting to get dark by now and the driver, after eying me suspiciously, lowered his window by a fraction of an inch.

"Hi," I said. "Could you tell me a little bit about the shelter here?" "Yeah," he said. "Whadya wanna know?"

"Well, is it well-run-- is it a safe place to stay?"

"It's alright. It depends on the group staying there and who's in charge. It's run by volunteers."

"Does it ever get rowdy?"

"Yeah-- sometimes."

"So what happens then-- do the volunteers kick people out?"

"Naw, they just lock themselves in the office."
I was taken aback. For a few moments I didn't know what to say. Then another thought crossed my mind.

"Do you feel it's safe to leave your car out here all night?"

"Yeah, you know why-- because we let it be known on the street that anybody who messes with our vehicles will end up in the hospital."
This was not turning out the way I thought it would. I thanked him curtly and went on my way. "Strike Two," I said to myself.

By this time it was totally dark, and when I drove back to the city shelter that was now lit by outside lighting, I noticed there were people lining up by the door at the end of the building. After parking my van, I got at the end of the line and waited. About fifteen minutes later the door opened and a person, whom I figured was the shelter supervisor, started checking I.D.'s and letting people in. When my turn came I was allowed in, but told to wait in the supervisor's office since this was my first night and the required forms had to be filled out. The office was small with a standard metal desk, a few chairs, some filing cabinets, and a mini-fridge. There was also a single folded-up cot that (I later learned) the supervisor would sleep on for the night. As I waited for him to return, I noticed a whiff of disinfectant in the air-- not a pleasant odor, but under the circumstances, reassuring. Larry, the supervisor, soon returned and after checking my Connecticut driver's license and filling out the required forms, led me back to the dormitory where I was allowed to choose a cot and a locker. After being issued fresh sheets, a blanket, and a bath towel, I was shown the bathroom facilities. They looked clean and well-maintained which further reassured me. There was just enough time for me to wash up and return to my cot for "lights out" at 10:30 PM.

As I was lying on my cot and staring towards the ceiling, the reality of my situation hit me with full force. Here I was, less than a month from my 58th birthday, forced to stay in a homeless shelter and it was all the result of my own stupid, careless lack of financial planning-- I had no one to blame but *myself.* And with that depressing thought in mind, I quietly cried myself to sleep.

"OK-- time to get up. Let's go everybody," boomed a loud voice, as bright neon light flooded the room. It was 6:30 AM, and everyone had exactly two hours to get washed, dressed, and complete his assigned chores before the dormitory would be locked at 8:30 AM, and remain so until 9 PM that night. In theory, two hours was more than enough time to do this, but in practice it never seemed that way. I quickly learned you had to make every minute count (more on this later). My first morning's routine was thankfully easy because I hadn't been assigned any chores yet, so there was plenty of time for me to get to the soup kitchen before it closed at 9 AM.

My previous day's experience at the Dorothy Day shelter had left me wondering if its soup kitchen counterpart would be something equally unpleasant, but fortunately it would not be the case. I found the food and atmosphere (though nothing to write home about) good enough the first morning, and all the other times I ended up eating there. In fact the only surprises that the place would ever give me concerning food were positive. For example I remember once being served shrimp, and another time, wedding cake, both items most likely donated leftovers from special events.

The main issue with the soup kitchen, as I quickly learned, was not the food but timing your arrival so that (A), you wouldn't have to wait in line and (B), once admitted, have to put up with one of the staff (usually the same gruff man whom I had met the first day) hovering nearby, pestering you to hurry up and finish eating so somebody else who was standing in line could take your place. To avoid these annoyances, I would try to arrive about 20 minutes before the official closing time when there was usually no longer a waiting line. I said "official" closing time because if you were still sitting and eating when the door was locked, the kitchen staff would let you stay an additional 10-15 minutes while they were cleaning up, and they rarely bothered you in the meantime. Arriving late like this increased the chances of them running out of a particular menu item, but this almost never happened and if it did, they would offer you something else in its place.

So ended my first night at the city homeless shelter and the morning after. I felt that I had made the right choice in shelters, and now I just had to acclimate myself to my new "home" and its other residents.

Part II

Basic Facilities
The Acclimation Process
My Fellow Residents

Establishing a bearable daily routine for myself while sleeping (or trying to sleep) each night in a homeless shelter required some improvisation on my part. To better explain why, I must first briefly describe the shelter's basic facilities. The only outside entrance to the dormitories was at the end of the building, the same entrance that we were admitted through every night. It led directly into the men's dormitory room with 12-15 cots, while the smaller women's dormitory room (5 cots) and separate bathroom were accessed through the men's side, then around the corner to the left. Towards the opposite end of the men's dorm there were two doors; the left one led to the hallway that connected the front entrance to the director's office and community room; the right one led directly into the men's bathroom. This bathroom consisted of the following fixtures; along the wall immediately to the right of the door were four sinks with mirrors, and along the opposite wall were (left to right) a single urinal, three shower stalls with plastic curtains and finally, in its own small alcove, a single toilet with no curtain or barrier to offer any privacy.

Leaving out the more optional features like shower stalls and sinks, and focusing on just the single toilet and urinal; then keeping in mind how many residents on average (10-12) would be trying to use them at about the same time each morning, gives a sense of what I would describe as the bathroom's "morning mad scramble". It was semi-chaotic to say the least, and about a half-hour after it started there would be three or four more people added to the mix, each trying to complete his assigned bathroom chore while working around everyone else who was still in there. (This is why I used to dread the mornings when I was assigned a bathroom chore like cleaning the shower stalls or mopping the floor. It was much better to be outside sweeping up cigarette butts, rain or shine, with nobody there to get in your way, taking up valuable time). But soon my body began to adjust to the new reality that on most mornings the best I could hope for in the shelter bathroom would be a visit to the urinal and a quick face wash, not necessarily in that order. I had to find either a less hectic time of day to use the shelter bathroom, or else find other places altogether to take care of my bodily needs. I ended up doing both.

I soon learned that the shelter bathroom in the 30-45 minute period before lights out at 10:30 PM was an entirely different place than in the morning. There would rarely be more than two other people in there besides myself. I could leisurely shower, shave and use the more basic facilities, although sitting on a toilet in plain sight was never 100% comfortable, even when I was the only person in the room. The period between when the shelter dorm closed at 8:30 AM and when it re-opened again at 9

PM was more than twelve hours, so during the day I had to find other places "to go". Perched on a knoll overlooking a broad bend in I-84 is an upscale motor inn. In its lobby there is a spotlessly clean restroom that I would end up using on a regular basis, but never two days in a row. There were similar facilities around the city that I would use the same way.

Sleep was another bodily need I had to be careful about during my shelter stay. For that entire period I could count on one hand the number of times I got a good night's sleep. This was more my fault than the shelter's-- the variety of background noises produced by ten or more people sleeping in a confined space always bothered me, although ear plugs helped somewhat. Being overtired a lot increased the chances of my getting sick, and that was my greatest fear-- not being assaulted, because once sick I wouldn't have even been allowed to stay in the shelter. So on most days I had to be sure to take at least one nap, usually in the afternoon but not always. Finding safe locations to do this was vital. A library was usually a good place for napping as long as I could find an empty chair in an inconspicuous location. I started doing this in the city library, till one day I was awakened by a tap on the knee and a security guard standing over me. "You can't sleep here," he said quietly. So I apologized, and soon moved on to more secure napping grounds, the upper floors of the WestConn library. There I managed to doze many times without ever being interrupted.

Dozing in a sitting position is one thing, but sleeping while lying down is infinitely better. One day I got the idea of using the chaise-lounge that was folded up in the back of my minivan. But where to do it safely took some thought. Tarrywile was a former estate that was turned into a park after being donated to the City of Danbury. There was a manor house and beautiful landscaped grounds, both of which could be rented out for special events like craft fairs or wedding receptions. The grounds however were open to the public most of the time. I don't remember when I first thought of driving up there, but I'm glad I did because it turned out to be the best napping location of them all.

On my first visit I drove into the upper parking lot which was surrounded by the neatly mowed grounds to the rear of the manor house. Among the inviting features there was a small grove of crabapple trees just feet away from the driveway leading in. I parked at the far end of the lot from the main house, then set up my chaise-lounge on the edge of the lawn next to my van so that I was partially shielded from view. It was mid-morning on a weekday and I had the place to myself. After actually *sleeping* for about an hour, I opened my eyes to a truly idyllic scene-- no more than 40 feet away was a small herd of deer grazing beneath the crabapple trees. Every few moments one of them would raise its head, listen, then continue grazing. Apparently they hadn't noticed me yet, so I did my best to remain perfectly quiet and still. Watching those deer for what seemed like forever put me into an entirely different state of mind. All my worries disappeared, and I felt so at peace and just living in the moment. Eventually one of them raised its tail as a warning, then bolted into the woods with the others close behind. I then closed my eyes and thanked God for what I had experienced. *It was moments like these that kept me going.* I would return to this location frequently until the weather became too hot Each visit would be nice and there would be more deer sightings too, but none of these trips would be quite as memorable as the first one.

Getting into a bearable daily routine in the shelter and establishing a plan of action to get out of there were not mutually exclusive tasks. Rather they both unfolded at about the same time, not always smoothly but good enough to keep me optimistic. After talking with a social worker at the shelter and others, I decided that the best course of action would be to apply for admission to a local group home that was well-known and respected. Once there I could hopefully sleep better and start looking for work. Early on I was interviewed by the home's acting director who said that she would recommend me to the admissions committee. About six weeks later I was approved for admission, but had to wait until an opening became available since they only had room for a limited number of people. In the meantime I would carry on with my daily routine, and in the process get to know some of my fellow shelter residents better.

All the residents that I got to know at least a little bit can be categorized into two main groups; regulars and floaters. A regular was someone who stayed almost every night for weeks, and possibly months to the point where his occasional absence would be noticed immediately and commented upon. A floater, on the other hand, would stay for a while, leave, then return once more to begin the cycle again. The timing of these arrivals and departures would depend on a variety of reasons; the time of month, the weather, and the current available space at the privately-run shelters nearby. As a general rule most floaters would show up and leave as a group, although there could be noted individual exceptions to this pattern. All the other shelter residents who were there when I was could be lumped into one remaining, broad category-- temps. A temp was a person who stayed no more than a few days or maybe a week at most before leaving, never to be seen again. I have little or no memory of the temps because of how quickly most of them moved on. When I first arrived I thought of myself as one, but as things turned out I ended up being a regular instead.

The regulars consisted of the following individuals: Marlboro Man, Bullpen Coach, Marathon Runner, Cool Dude, Ornery One, and Gold Coast Doc. What follows is a brief description of each one.

Marlboro Man bore an uncanny resemblance to one of the cowboys featured in the old Marlboro cigarette commercial. Although he never wore an actual Stetson, his customary wide-brimmed hat was close enough and it, along with his handlebar mustache and rolling gait, couldn't help but make me think "cowboy". He was also a heavy smoker which enhanced this image. I never did learn what his favorite brand of cigarettes was, or if he had one. His quiet, self-confident manner somehow gave me the impression that he was originally from the country, and was used to working outdoors. I found out later that he was indeed from a rural area and had worked on a farm. I never heard him say anything nor see him do anything to cause trouble with any staff member or resident.

Bullpen Coach was tall, lanky, and always wore a baseball-style cap pushed back halfway with the visor facing forward. He seemed to have an encyclopedic knowledge of major league baseball pitchers and all the ups and downs of their careers. I couldn't envisage him as a pitcher though, because he was obviously past his prime and wouldn't have lasted a single inning. When he wasn't hanging around the shelter, chatting and smoking with Marlboro Man, I would often see him shuffling along New Street either on his way to or coming from the city library (most likely place) as if he had all the time in the world.

Marathon Runner, on the other hand, kept himself busy between washing laundry for the shelter and his passion for long-distance running. He was probably the most physically-fit person in the place and would almost never call off his daily 2+ mile run, regardless of the weather. Friendly and deeply religious, he would prove to be a reliable source of information as to what was happening around the shelter and soup kitchen.

Cool Dude was aloof, observant, and oh-so cool. He was in the habit of using the phrase "mother f*****g b***h" so often that I regarded it as his "linguistic signature". Whenever I heard those words faintly in the distance, I instantly knew where he probably was without having to look.

Ornery One could also be called Most Disliked, not only because of how irascible he usually was, but also due to his self-appointed role as shelter busybody/spy/snitch, with an emphasis on the last aspect. Informing the supervisor of a violation that virtually guaranteed a suspension gave Ornery One great pleasure which he would often later express in front of the affected person. Another one of his annoying habits was to lurk near the shelter office door in the hope of eavesdropping on a conversation (or a snippet of one) between the director and a particular resident. And if his efforts were successful, he would advertise it by saying something revealing to the person (like me) he had spied on. I considered him to be more of a nuisance than a threat; however his obnoxiousness always ran the risk of provoking violent reactions from some of the others.

Gold Coast Doc was a recent medical school graduate who nevertheless had fallen on hard times. Gold Coast refers to where he was from; the Gold Coast of Connecticut, lower Fairfield County, the richest section of the richest county in one of the richest states per capita. I found him to be friendly and polite, the type of person I was tempted to ask, "What's a person like you doing in a place like this?" Before I got up the nerve to do so however, someone else did as I was standing nearby and the Doc's cryptic answer was, "I had some bad luck with money and women." I used to see him working in the soup kitchen till one day he was gone, presumably moving on to bigger and better things in the world of medicine.

The floaters consisted of the following individuals: Feisty Kid, Helpful Harry, The Blustery Gent, Surly Kid, Sidekick, and The Bitten Lady. What follows is a brief description of each one.

Feisty Kid was tall and lean without a spare ounce of fat on his muscular frame. There were bulging veins along the length of sinewy arms, and etched on the middle of each bicep was a barbed-wire tattoo armband. With his large backpack casually slung over one shoulder, he looked to be in the prime of life. His outgoing manner was engaging at first, but soon his constant fidgeting, chain-smoking and milling around began to get on my nerves. He was definitely "wired"-- the only question was, "On what?" "I hope it's just coffee," I said to myself, and let it go at that.

Helpful Harry was memorable in several ways; he was always in a good mood, he was one of the few shelter residents who had his own vehicle, he had a $20-per-hour job at a local assembly plant (how I envied him), and lastly, he was the most obvious alcoholic in the place. More often than not I could smell alcohol on him from a few feet away, unlike most of the others with alcohol-issues who were more discreet. Their drink of choice was vodka which tended to be odorless, or so they thought. But Harry found ingenious ways to mask his alcoholic breath so that he was rarely refused entry to the dorm. He would later let me use his car for something that I had to do.

The Blustery Gent was by far the most memorable resident, "a character" to be sure. By the way he dressed and acted it seemed as though he was always trying to send us all a message such as, "Look at me. I have been places and done things. I deserve your attention and respect." First of all, he was physically imposing-- roughly 6.5 feet tall, with a large graying head, a high forehead, intelligent eyes, a roman nose, and a mustache reminiscent of an old-time movie star. His clothes were eye-catching as well, a unique blend of the formal and practical-- mostly formal from the waist up, and purely practical from the waist down. His favorite headwear was a khaki bush hat with an extra wide brim, although in cooler weather he would switch to a black ski cap. He generally wore a dark gray sport coat over a dress shirt with the collar unbuttoned, and in chilly weather he would also drape over his shoulders a long thick scarf, emblazoned with an impressive coat-of-arms. From the waist down, regardless of the weather, he wore khaki Bermuda shorts and tall yellow hiking boots, each tightly laced with a bright-red sock cuff neatly folded over the top. His favorite pastime was regaling anyone who was willing to listen with tales of his exploits, some real and others exaggerated no doubt. A deep resonant voice, a hearty laugh, and a flair for dramatic gesturing all helped to make him a captivating storyteller. I would learn through experience that his urge to entertain was more like a compulsion which he sometimes had little or no control over.

Surly Kid was tall, husky, and even on his good days, slightly menacing due largely to his reputation and customary facial expression that varied little from insolent to surly--merely insolent to those in authority like shelter supervisors, and downright surly to those of his peers whom he may have felt like intimidating. His impulsive and rebellious nature would lead to his numerous suspensions. (A suspension from the city shelter usually lasted no more than 3 days). He was almost always accompanied by his best friend, Sidekick. As one staff member once told me, "The two of them seemed to be joined at the hip." Whenever either one was staying in the shelter, I was slightly on edge and I'm sure there were others who felt the same way.

Sidekick was lanky and sullen-- an inwardly meaner but outwardly less intimidating version of his best friend. Unlike Surly Kid, he usually stayed out of trouble, although he would occasionally vent his spleen over his best friend's latest suspension by kicking a plastic garbage can across the shelter's community room (close to lights out when hardly anyone was there).

Of all the faces I remember from my shelter stay, hers was the one that affected me the most. From her shapely figure and luxuriant blondish hair, I could tell that The Bitten Lady had once been an attractive woman. But her face now told a much different story-- her facial features were slightly distorted in a grotesque way to the point where it was difficult for me to look at them for more than a few moments without cringing. I had never seen anything like it-- in real life anyway. Her appearance reminded me of a victim from one of those old time horror movies, after she had been bitten by the monster/zombie/vampire. Such a bite wouldn't kill her, or make her unrecognizable to her friends and loved ones, but would merely distort her facial features just enough to let them know that she had been preyed upon. What I was seeing though was no make-believe character from a movie, but a real person, suffering the effects of real-life substance abuse. With some effort I probably could have learned more about her, perhaps what substances she had abused and might still be doing so, but why go to the trouble if the result would only make me cringe more? I already had a general idea of what they were so I didn't spend any more time on it. There were other residents who bore the marks of substance abuse, but none did so as vividly as The Bitten Lady.

Part III

Blustery Gent Drama

A Soup Kitchen Encounter

An Unforeseen Exit

Where Have All The Floaters Gone

I first experienced The Blustery Gent's talkative nature in an unusual place. It happened on one of the first few mornings of my stay while I was trying to shave in the bathroom, before I knew better than to try and do anything so time-consuming during the bathroom's "morning mad scramble". I noticed the person who was using the sink next to me on the right had, to his right, The Blustery Gent who was busy talking to him. I didn't pay much attention to it because I had a problem of my own to deal with. All three showers were in use, and even with the bathroom window open all the way, the billowing steam being generated was constantly fogging all the sink mirrors. I tried wiping my mirror several times, but it would just fog again within seconds. Suddenly the person to my right was gone and in his place, looming over me, stood The Blustery Gent.

He smiled and began to speak. Throughout his presentation he never restrained nor even touched me once. He didn't have to-- like the Ancient Mariner, he held me with his glittering eye. The gist of his story was this. Back in the 1980's he was the newly-appointed director of a local non-profit organization. Things were a mess, the place was going downhill fast-- that is, until he took charge. Although the obstacles facing him were many and appeared to be insurmountable at first, he persevered nevertheless and slowly but surely turned the place around, till once again it regained its sound financial footing. His speech was riveting, complete with dramatic gestures and pauses at timely moments. Throughout all of it I hardly said a word-- just nodded my head at key intervals, with an occasional "uh huh" added for emphasis. As he was finally wrapping up his story, I shifted my gaze slightly upward, away from his face, to the clouds of steam billowing around his head. I then had to bite my lip to keep from laughing, because from where I was standing it looked like the steam was coming *from* his head. A few moments later, he abruptly turned and left me alone amidst the steam. Well, not quite alone, for I could see now that one of the shower-takers had finished and was standing with a towel wrapped around him. He must have heard at least some of what was said because when he looked at me, he just rolled his eyes and shook his head in disbelief. This gave me a good laugh which I didn't have to stifle.

I would have no more dramatic encounters in the bathroom. My laughter had been mostly a nervous reaction to strange behavior in an unusual setting. I was probably more unsettled by what had happened than I cared to admit. Apparently The Blustery Gent had "recordings" inside him that had to be played, regardless of the time or place. This would not be the last time I would witness his erratic nature.

While staying in the shelter and experiencing mostly periods of calm and even monotony, I would be reminded from time to time that the unpredictable was always lurking nearby. One such reminder occurred outside the soup kitchen one evening. To best explain what happened I must first briefly describe the soup kitchen's layout. Passing through the front entrance brings you into the first room which is narrow and deep, and contains primarily the kitchen, although immediately to the right by the front windows there's a circular dining table with space for about ten people. Just beyond this table, and to the left, is the only entrance to the second room which is the main dining area. Both rooms have windows looking out on Spring Street, and the front entrance door is essentially a clear-glass window set within a wooden door frame. There were advantages and disadvantages to sitting in either room; the main dining area (generally my preference) gave you a little more peace and quiet because of its distance from the kitchen, while the circular table in the kitchen room gave you a better chance of being served quicker.

On this particular evening the place was packed and I was forced to sit at the circular table, facing the kitchen with my back to the street. During the meal I happened to notice one of the kitchen workers, a tall husky man, standing near our table but not doing anything, which seemed unusual. After a closer look, I realized he was busy watching something going on outside behind me. He would squint, crane his neck one way, then the other, and start over again. Other people at our table began to notice him as well. Suddenly he grimaced and blurted out, "Oh s**t-- he's down!" Then looking straight at me, and anyone else at the table he could make eye contact with he added, "If anybody comes around asking questions just say he slipped and fell." Whatever it was that he had seen, I wasn't about to take any chances by going outside too soon.

So I took my time, finished my meal and then, after hearing an ambulance pull up, decided it was safe to leave. I had learned early on that dialing 911 in Danbury for an ambulance brought at least one police car and a fire engine too. As I was leaving a voice said, "Don't step in the blood," and I was grateful because it kept me from stepping into a pool of blood that was several inches wide just outside the front door. Turning around for another look, I heard a "splash" and the blood was gone-- instantly washed away by a cauldron of steaming hot water dumped squarely on target by the same kitchen worker who had seen everything. A freshly rinsed patch of asphalt was not much to gawk at compared to a pool of blood. "Move along now, nothing to see here." Those words were never actually spoken but everyone acted like he had heard them. We all moved along, the emergency vehicles drove away, and life on Spring Street quickly returned to normal.

I learned later that the victim had said something bad to Surly Kid who then punched him in the face. I never heard of any charges being filed or how seriously he had been hurt-- hopefully not too bad. I never did get a good look at him. By the time I went outside he was already in the ambulance. Being on the edge of something like this made me appreciate more the calm and sometimes boring periods of daily shelter life. And whenever I was tempted to wish for a little more excitement around the place, I would stop myself immediately by thinking, "Remember. Here, boring is good......yes.......boring is good!"

Not long after the encounter outside the soup kitchen there was another surprise, this time in the dorm itself. One night after lights out as I was still trying to get to sleep, I heard someone get up and go into the bathroom. This was not unusual, and I thought nothing of it at first. But what happened next caused quite a stir. "Hey Larry-- somebody threw up in here," a voice cried out in disgust. The dorm was soon brightly lit as Larry, the dorm supervisor for the night, came in from where he had been sleeping in the office to survey the mess. From where I was stretched out on my cot (a good 20-25 feet away) I couldn't see anything even with the lights on, and I wasn't about to get up for a closer look. Then I got a whiff of a disgusting odor and thought, "My God, if I can smell it

over here, how much worse it must be for those close up."
To Larry's credit he and at least one other person went to work immediately. The outside door was propped open, along with the bathroom door and window, to create a cool and refreshing flow of night air from one end of the dorm to the other. The mess soon disappeared in a flurry of mops, buckets and disinfectant-- then the time came for Larry to confront the person who was responsible for it.

I propped my head up slightly to get a good profile view of the culprit who was sitting on his cot in front of Larry, near the bathroom door. It was Surly Kid. He was looking rather sheepish now, a far cry from his usual demeanor but what really caught my eye was the greenish tint to his complexion, a phenomenon that I had never seen before. After a short pause, Larry began to speak to him in a calm, almost apologetic tone of voice.

"You know you can't stay here tonight because you're sick. You have to leave. If I let you stay it wouldn't be fair to everybody else here who isn't sick."

There was no reaction.

"Do you want me to call an ambulance?"

This time there was a head shake meaning, "no."

"Do you want me to call the police?"

This provoked a greater head shake, "no."

"Do you need any help getting out?"

There was a third and final head shake, "no."

Then the Kid staggered to his feet and began to demonstrate how drunk he really was. He couldn't walk down the middle of the room to the outside door that was still propped open. Instead, he had to take a more indirect route by first staggering over to the nearest wall, then using it like a crutch by stumbling against it repeatedly as he slowly made his way down the length of the dorm. And since this entire wall was lined with full-size metal lockers, his constant stumbling against them made quite a racket, so I could gauge his progress by sound alone without bothering to look. But after closing my eyes and hearing the noise grow louder, I suddenly realized (to my horror) his projected route would bring him to within three feet of where I was comfortably resting my head. A quick glance to either side showed that nobody else was moving an inch, so I decided to take my chances too. I closed my eyes and said a silent prayer; "Please God, don't let this person trip and fall on top of me.......or worse." As the noise grew louder, then reached a crescendo, I held my breath-- then as it gradually decreased, I exhaled a long, deep sigh of relief. And as it finally died away completely, I turned my head just in time to see the Kid staggering out the doorway and into the misty night. "Thank God," I said to myself as I tried to get some sleep at last.

During the following afternoon I began to wonder about how he had made out. The night had been a little chilly but not dangerously cold, and if it had been then I'm sure an ambulance would have been called, regardless of his feelings. Apparently he had managed to reach a friend's apartment nearby where he was allowed to "crash" for the night. His unforeseen exit was not only a reminder of how important it was to stay healthy, but also of what it took to be a good dorm supervisor.

After a couple of months in the shelter, I began to notice how the occupancy rate would fluctuate from full or almost to full, to about half-full on a fairly regular basis. Full occupancy was fifteen for men and five for women. Since most of the women were friends of some of the men, the occupancy rate for both groups tended to rise and fall together. The changing occupancy rate was a mixed blessing for the regulars like me who stayed put. Having fewer people around made the dorm less crowded and allowed for easier access to the bathroom, but it also meant there were fewer people available to do the same number of required chores. I didn't mind this very much because none of the chores were too hard, and I never saw or heard of anyone being reprimanded for not doing them well enough. I enjoyed having less people around because it was usually the more potentially disruptive ones who were missing. These were the floaters, the ones who moved from shelter to shelter (and other places) on a regular basis. During one of the quiet periods while they were away, I began wondering where they were and what they might be doing. There was a rumor going around about a location on abandoned railroad property called "the place" where some of them would meet and get high on whatever controlled substances they preferred to use or, in some cases, *had* to use. Although I heard this from more than one source, I never had (or wanted to have) the chance to confirm it. A casual conversation one day with Marathon Runner gave me another possible insight into their behavior.

According to him, their movements were largely determined by how quickly they spent their monthly stipend. Apparently a lot of them were receiving some type of government aid that arrived at or shortly after the beginning of each month. Then as the month progressed, and the money began to run out as they spent it, sometimes wisely but oftentimes not, they would gravitate back to the city shelter which was the cheapest place to stay. The private shelters charged fees that weren't much, but when the money's running out "not much" can be a lot. "So why don't they stay here in the city shelter all the time?" I asked him. "Because they have to do chores here. The other places give them more freedom," was his response. I could never prove that what he said was true, but I did notice the city shelter tended to have the highest occupancy rate towards the end of the month, and the lowest after the first week.

The Blustery Gent seemed to chafe the most at any restrictions on his freedom. He seemed to be the most independent of the floaters, and would often regale us with tales of his solo adventures in the Big Apple where he would sometimes visit a "massage parlor" as he described it, with a wink and a nod. Another time someone asked him where he had been lately, and he answered, "I've been visiting the Blessed Lady but I have to leave before Her worshippers arrive." This sounded like gibberish at first, till I realized later he was probably referring to his camping out on the grounds of a local Roman Catholic shrine.

As the weather got warmer, he wasn't the only one who started camping out. I remember one morning as I was taking out the garbage, being startled by a rustling sound in the high grass near the dumpster. I jumped back a few feet, expecting an animal to rush out at me. Instead it was a person slowly getting up from a mat where he had slept the previous night, someone who may have been refused entry to the shelter.

For all their adventures and antics, the floaters were some of the most hardcore homeless, and it slowly dawned on me that for some of them there would be no recovery. This would be how they would spend the rest of their lives. And I tried not to think about it too much.

Part IV

A Discreet Meeting Goes Noticed

Helpful Harry Lends A Car

Heat Wave Blues

Living Dangerously In Close Quarters

A Dispute In The Dorm

Good News At Last

Around the beginning of June I was already more than half-way through my shelter experience, although I didn't know it at the time. I still had not received word about when space would be available in the group home that had accepted me, so in the meantime I continued to wait and observe daily life in the shelter. Not everything that I remember was obviously noteworthy or dramatic. Once there was something so low-key and un-dramatic that I probably would have missed if I had been even slightly preoccupied at the time. To explain what I mean, I must first briefly describe the city shelter's immediate surroundings.

The driveway leading into the shelter is easy to miss because there is no sign out front that indicates where it leads to. It's also quite narrow, sandwiched between a concrete wall and a plastic fence, and has room for one-way traffic only. If two vehicles meet, the one going out usually backs up first because it's safer than forcing the other to back onto New Street. Just before reaching the left end of the shelter, about 150 feet in from New Street, the driveway makes a 90 degree turn to the right, and as it passes along the length of the building, gradually widens into a parking lot. This small parking area to the right side of the shelter has marked spaces for several standard-size vehicles to be parked side-by-side in single file. Both the shelter building and parking lot are tucked at the base of a near-vertical escarpment that a mountain goat would have trouble climbing. Immediately beyond the end of the parking lot, there is just enough level ground to fit a large dumpster and not much more. This is because of a drainage gully that runs along the front edge of the parking lot and then curves around to the base of the escarpment, leaving only a narrow strip of level ground beyond the dumpster. However, on this bit of ground there was once a narrow footpath that led to a small, dense thicket of entwined vines and brush.

What I almost didn't notice happened on a typical early evening as we were waiting for the dorm to open. It was warm with about a half-hour of daylight remaining. Our group had broken into three or four circles of smoking and chatting in the parking lot. As I was standing there, a woman whom I had never seen before sauntered by, and without saying a word to anyone, continued to the end of the parking lot, past the dumpster, then along the narrow footpath, before disappearing into the thicket. Hardly anyone seemed to notice, probably because there was nothing about her to readily attract attention. Although tall and somewhat attractive, she was wearing nothing out of the ordinary-- just a blouse with blue jeans and sandals. But what I found interesting was how she seemed to know exactly where to go without the slightest hesitation whatsoever. About ten minutes later Sidekick sauntered by, and without saying a word to anyone, retraced the woman's route, before he too disappeared into the thicket. At that moment I had to shake my head in amazement, marveling at the nerve and ingenuity it took to pull off a stunt like this in such confined surroundings and in front of so many potential witnesses. I said "potential" because nobody else there seemed to notice anything, except Cool Dude. He was busy going from circle to circle, asking repeatedly, "Did you catch what that mother f*****g b***h just did?......"Did you catch what that mother f*****g b***h just did?" But his efforts were in vain as everyone's attention was immediately diverted by the opening of the dorm. Soon we began filing in, as Sidekick and his companion had yet to finish whatever it was they were up to inside the thicket.

About this time I seriously considered becoming a postal mail carrier. In order to qualify I had to pass a

USPS-administered driving test, part of which involved having to park a vehicle perfectly between two painted lines in one try, with no vehicle parked in either adjacent space to act as a guide. I wasn't very good at this so I needed to practice beforehand. Another incentive to practice was knowing that if I failed the test, I would have to wait a minimum of six months before being allowed to retake it. I had the choice of being tested with my own vehicle or with one that the postal service would provide. Since my minivan was not in great shape, I thought it best to use their vehicle which I was told would be either a two or four-door sedan. I soon came up with a plan.

Helpful Harry drove a four-door sedan and the shelter parking lot would be an ideal location to practice parking because over half of its marked spaces were empty most of the time-- plus I wouldn't have to drive his car somewhere else, or worse yet, have *him* drive his car somewhere else with me as a passenger. When I told him about my plan he readily agreed to help. But first I needed time to learn the correct parking technique. After doing some online research at the library and talking to an instructor at a local driving school, I found out it was easier than I thought-- you use the door mirrors to locate certain reference points that indicate when and how much to turn the wheel. After practicing some with my van, I told Harry I was ready to try it with his car. I had to wait though, because at this point he wasn't staying in the shelter on a regular basis.

One day without warning as I was standing in the shelter parking lot, he pulled up next to me and said, "OK Guy-- let's do this right now." I could smell alcohol on him from six feet away. He got out of the car and went around to sit in the front passenger's seat while I got behind the wheel. Even with all four side windows rolled down his car smelled of alcohol. As I shifted into gear he stopped me by saying, "Wait a minute, I have to do something first." He turned away, towards a young woman who was hanging around the shelter and called out to her, "Hey baby—howya been? Long time no see. Comeer a minute. I wanna talk to ya. "She came over, they talked, and then he coaxed her into the back seat directly behind him with a reassuring, "Don't worry, we're not going anywhere-- he just wants to practice parking." I had a vague idea about whom this person might be, but dismissed it because of how pathetic-looking she was. I was also a little annoyed with Harry by now but didn't want to say anything that might antagonize him. So I focused on what I had to do-- practice parking so I could pass a driver's test. At first I was sloppy, but after a few tries got better to the point where I could do it right almost without thinking.

Then Harry dropped a bombshell. Turning around to the young woman he said, "Hey, let's cut to the chase baby-- what do I have to do to get you to polish my knob?" I gasped, then braced myself for what I thought was coming next-- the sound of Harry being slapped good 'n hard across the mouth. But what I heard next was worse. "You don't have to do anything. You just have to pay me," said the young woman in a calm, matter-of-fact tone of voice. I was shocked and thought, "So she is a hooker after all-- probably a novice, judging by the looks of her. *This is just what I need right now*-- Harry in the front seat, propositioning a hooker-novice sitting in the back!" I went numb, but kept my parking routine going by rote as Harry and the woman continued their racy conversation. A minute or so later she told me to stop, so she could get out and talk to some of her friends. She quickly disappeared around the corner of the driveway and that was the last we ever saw of her.

When I finally turned to look at Harry, I got another surprise. *He was beaming at me.* "You know why I did all this?" he asked, sending over a gust of alcohol in the process. Still to numb to speak, I just shook my head. "I wanted to see if you could perform under pressure and you did-- you were great, you were golden!" *And he was right.* Then he playfully poked me in the shoulder and offered me a "high five" which I slowly returned. My numbness soon disappeared, and both of us put our heads back to have a really good laugh. So ended my parking practice with Helpful Harry.

The middle of June would mark the beginning of a heat wave that would last for most of the summer, with a few short breaks here and there. I had to cut short my visits to Tarrywile and concentrate on staying indoors at air-conditioned locations during the heat of the day. Towards evening the city shelter with its central A/C system offered welcome relief at first, but then the A/C broke down about a week later. That was rough.

Hanging on the wall in the dorm was a large circular thermometer that resembled a clock face with only the minute hand. On its circumference was a temperature scale with a number at every 10 degree interval. All these numbers were large enough to be easily read at a distance. I didn't pay much attention to this thermometer "clock" at first, but once the heat wave began, I started watching it closely to see if I could tell how accurate its readings really were. The A/C would never be turned on until 10:15 PM each night, when the outside door was finally shut and locked. So when the dorm was opened at 9 PM most of the time, the temperature inside would rise for a little more than an hour. It would read in the high 70's at first, then rise to the low 80's by 10:15 PM; after the A/C was turned on, it would quickly fall back to the mid-70's or lower. These readings were an accurate reflection of how I felt during the same period; first slightly uncomfortable, then more uncomfortable; and finally very comfortable after the A/C started up. While the A/C was broken, this thermometer would read in the mid to high 80's when the dorm was opened, then rise to the mid-90's by lights out. The temperature would then drop back during the night to the high 80's by morning.

There was some delay in getting the A/C fixed, so in the meantime the shelter got a large industrial fan to help keep us slightly more comfortable at least. This fan was about three feet in diameter, and had a heavy-duty, tubular steel frame and base to keep it mounted about six feet off the floor. I nicknamed it the B-52 fan because of its loud roar, a noise so loud that it drowned out all other sounds in the room, and actually made it a little easier for me to fall asleep. The airflow generated did make the dorm slightly more comfortable, but one night-- apparently due to the strength of its airflow-- the fan tipped over backwards with a crash, causing a big commotion. But after heavy objects were placed on its base, this never happened again.

The heat wave wasn't the only thing that I had to cope with at this time. There was also some disappointing news from the group home that had accepted me. Apparently the house now had room, but also had some maintenance issues crop up that required fixing before any new people could be admitted. The director apologized and reassured me that I wouldn't have to wait much longer. Though disappointed, I wasn't about to give up at this point. So my shelter stay dragged on, and I continued to keep my eyes and ears open to what was going on around me.

One of the people who made the shelter more bearable during the heat wave was Big Ike, a friendly but firm supervisor whose informal manner put everyone at ease. I remember him saying more than once, "This is the first job I've ever had that doesn't seem like a job." He would usually show up for work carrying a large dispenser-container of spring water with drinking cups for us all Another thing he liked to do was move the small desk that was used for signing people in (usually near the dorm entrance) to the middle of the room. There-- with him sitting on one end of the desk, the sign-in sheet in the middle and the spring water on the other end, he would chat with us while waiting for the remaining people to sign-in for the night.

One late afternoon, during a mini-break in the heat wave, he showed up earlier than usual and in addition to his customary routine, opened up enough doors and windows to allow a slight breeze through the dorm. After having a few cups of spring water, I stretched out on my cot and half-shut my eyes with nothing but the sounds of friendly conversation around me. All I wanted to do was enjoy the peacefulness of the moment without having to talk to anyone.

Then from out of nowhere Surly Kid appeared at Ike's side. As he was about to sign-in, Ike stopped him by saying, "Aren't you still under suspension?" The Kid didn't say a word, but his downcast look was answer enough. "Yaaaaaaaay," shouted Ornery One as he clapped his hands with glee. He then began to merrily sing the refrain from the classic Ray Charles song "Hit The Road Jack" while clapping to the rhythm. After doing this once more for good measure, he stopped and sat there grinning. For this impromptu performance he deserved the alias Malevolent Miracle Worker for how, in an instant, he had miraculously transformed the atmosphere in the dorm from peaceful and secure to extremely tense and potentially dangerous. The rest of us gasped, expecting the worst. I glanced nervously at Surly Kid to gauge his reaction. First he dropped his jaw, blinked and shook his head a few times as if to say, "What!" Then with his jaw firmly closed, he fixed a laser-like gaze on his detractor and smiled evilly, as if to say, "I'll get even with you later." And without saying a word he left the dorm. After the rest of us had let out a deep sigh of relief, Big Ike turned to Ornery One and said, "I'd be careful with him if I were you. He could really mess you up." "Well then I'll have him arrested," was the testy response. "Yeah, but that won't make your head feel any better after it hits the pavement," was Ike's final bit of advice. His husky presence had kept things under control.

This was the most extreme example of Ornery One's living dangerously that I witnessed. Soon afterwards he found permanent housing and left the shelter for good. I'm sure I wasn't the only one who was glad to see him go. I'm still amazed that despite his provocative behavior, he was never beaten up or even punched once. It's nothing short of miraculous.

The last bit of shelter drama that I would experience occurred during the worst part of the heat wave while the shelter's A/C system was still broken. On this particular evening Don, the supervisor for the night, didn't show up on time. Tempers were already short due to the heat, and his late arrival didn't help matters any. As we began to settle in for the night, I heard an argument break out between him and Feisty Kid. Apparently one of the Kid's friends, someone who had been admitted the previous night by another supervisor, had been denied entry this time by Don. I never did learn exactly why. This made the Kid angry because, as far as he could tell, there had been no change in his friend's sober condition to justify Don's refusal. Don was adamant-- he wouldn't change his mind. And the Kid wouldn't give up either-- amid much swearing he kept the argument going. The situation was spinning out of control.

Then to make matters worse, The Blustery Gent suddenly got involved. From out of the blue he appeared inches away from the Kid's face and yelled, "Don't you dare question my supervisor's decision!" I was standing by my locker about six feet from the action, and when I heard this I had to turn away to keep from laughing in front of both of them. For here was The Blustery Gent, the perennial thorn-in-the-side of every dorm supervisor, the one who always complained the most about shelter rules and regulations now suddenly defending *his* supervisor! It was too much. My turning away however prevented me from seeing what happened next. I heard sounds of a scuffle, cots being tossed about, and something hitting the floor. Quickly turning back I saw a dazed Blustery Gent on the floor while an agitated Feisty Kid, with clenched fists, danced around yelling, "He bit me-- didja see that, he bit me!" From my close vantage point I couldn't see a drop of blood on either one of them, so whatever the Kid was talking about it must have been more like a nip than an actual toothy bite. This marked the end of the scuffle because the Gent seemed to be in no mood to continue. In a clearing on the floor, surrounded by overturned cots, he was apparently unhurt and was now sitting, talking to himself. His legs were splayed out in front like a "V", and to maintain his sitting position he had a palm pressed to the floor on each side of him, slightly to the rear.

Don finally reacted to this melee by yelling at the Kid, "That's it-- pack up your s**t and get out!" But the Kid refused to leave-- he stood his ground and continued to argue. Finally Don had had enough. "OK-- I'm calling the police right now," he said as he started pushing buttons on his cell phone. Feisty Kid gave up at last. With a final burst of profanity he slung his backpack over his shoulder and stalked out. After his dramatic departure an uneasy murmur settled over the dorm. The Blustery Gent was still on the floor, cots were still scattered, and none of us knew exactly what would happen next.

A few minutes later two cops arrived and started chatting with Don. I noticed Surly Kid and Sidekick watching them intently. After what seemed like a long time, one of the cops jerked his thumb towards the Gent and asked Don, "So what do you want us to do with him?" "Naw, he stays," was Don's reply. Upon hearing this, both Surly Kid and Sidekick shook their heads in disbelief, and one said to the other, "If we did anything half as bad we'd be kicked out of here in two seconds." And with some reluctance I had to admit-- they did have a point. I learned later that because of his age and status as a veteran, The Blustery Gent *was* given preferential treatment, as were all veterans. I understand the rationale for this, and also why it caused some resentment among a few other residents.

What really struck me about this experience was how, given the right set of conditions and participants, a simple argument can escalate out of control so quickly. I originally blamed Don for not managing the situation better, but now I'm thinking that not even the best supervisor could have prevented what happened, because the elapsed time from when the argument began till when the Gent hit the floor was, in my estimation, no more than 60 seconds.

As the heat wave continued, the first bit of good news that we received one day came in the form of an A/C repairman's truck parked close to the shelter. We later found out that it would take several days for the A/C to be fixed because of how much extensive work needed to be done. It was going to be more like a system overhaul than a simple repair job. After talking each day with the repairmen, Bullpen Coach would brief us on how the work was progressing. To emphasize some of what he learned, he once held his thumb and index finger apart to indicate a space of about a half-inch as he told us, "One of the repairmen said there was *that much* dust and dirt on the evaporator and condenser coils." After we all shook our heads in disgust over this obvious neglect in maintenance, he added with great finality, "No wonder the A/C conked out." Waiting those last few days for the A/C to start up again was tough, but we were soon rewarded with a cool and comfortable dorm.

The other good news was that the group home director said I could move in now, but don't rush because the home had no central A/C system, just A/C window units in a few rooms. So I ended up spending a few extra nights in the shelter by choice because of the heat wave. When I first arrived I expected to be there no more than a month, but the unexpected length of my stay and the heat was wearing me down. I was starting to make careless mistakes, one of which could have been costly but for the kindness of a fellow resident.

Close to my last night there I took a shower and left my shorts with my wallet near the shower stall. Before I had even realized it I heard a voice by my cot saying, "You left this in the bathroom-- you gotta be careful in this place." *It was Surly Kid of all people.* He handed me my shorts and before I had a chance to thank him, he turned around and went back into the bathroom. I checked my wallet-- nothing was missing. He was the last person in the place whom I would have thought capable of doing such a good deed. Maybe he wasn't so bad after all.

My last night in the shelter was so anticlimactic that I don't remember anything about it or the next morning either, until I pulled into the driveway of the group home. Soon after arriving there I was glad to learn that the first task in store for me was to help install additional A/C window units throughout the house, including the bedroom where I would be sleeping. So the first day in my new home was a little hot and sweaty at first, but got progressively cooler and more comfortable with each additional A/C unit that I helped to put up. My assigned bedroom was technically semi-private but the other person whom I would be sharing it with would not arrive for several days, so in the meantime I had the room to myself. After showering that first night and getting into my own twin bed (not a cot) I remember thinking how grateful I was to *finally* be here. It truly felt like the worst was over, and things would only get better from now on. I was too tired and emotionally drained to cry like I did during my first night in the shelter, but I do remember a few tears welling up as I drifted off to sleep.

Epilogue

I never fully appreciated what the term "safety net" meant until the day came when I had to seek help from it myself. In the process I learned both some good and bad news related to it.

The good news is that the safety net was there for me in 2011 when I needed it, and was staffed by compassionate people who did their jobs reasonably well. This was true in both the homeless shelter and soup kitchen, and later in the group home too. I'm grateful to all those people and particularly to Mike Flynn (his real name), the director of the shelter while I was there. Any bad first impressions that I may have received from some of the privately-run shelters should not be used to disparage the good work that they have done, and hopefully continue to do. A bad first impression can be just that, and nothing more. As for the City of Danbury itself-- I ended up living and working there full-time for the next several years and found it to be, on the whole, a safe and friendly place.

The bad news is that the best safety net in the world cannot adequately help those who refuse to be helped-- those individuals who simply will not or cannot deviate from the self-destructive lifestyles they are following. I was reminded of this several months after I had started working full-time, on the day that I visited the New Milford soup kitchen. I had heard good things about it and wanted to see what it was like for myself. The food was excellent and the staff were very friendly.

As I was leaving I noticed a tall figure who looked vaguely familiar. He was slightly hunched over his food and seemed to be in a trance. Unshaven and disheveled, he was a sorry sight. As I walked in front of where he was sitting, he looked up at me and nodded slightly. It was The Blustery Gent, and as soon as I recognized him a shiver went down my spine. I never knew if he actually recognized me because I was too unnerved to speak to him, something I now regret. Maybe what he was going through was only temporary and he would soon be back to his old vibrant self-- at least that's what I told myself at the time. But even if it were true, the homeless nomadic life he seemed compelled to lead would catch up with him eventually. And it makes me sad to think that he and others like him are beyond the point the point of no return.

Addendum On Shelter Regulations

Here is additional information about how well some of the more important shelter regulations were observed and enforced. A particular regulation will be listed, followed by pertinent commentary.

DOORS OPEN FOR SIGN-IN AT 9:00 PM.

This was true most of the time; however there were a few evenings when the scheduled supervisor forgot that he was on duty and arrived more than an hour late. This happened once on a cold and windy night. But during the summer heat wave, Big Ike would routinely show up almost an hour early.

ALCOHOL AND DRUGS ARE NOT ALLOWED ON THE PREMISES.

This rule was strictly enforced and I was never aware of anyone breaking it. One evening a few Danbury police officers showed up with a drug-sniffing dog to search the dorm, but no drugs were found.

STAFF RESERVES THE RIGHT TO DENY YOU ENTRANCE IF THEY DETERMINE YOU ARE UNDER THE INFLUENCEOF DRUGS AND/OR ALCOHOL.

This meant that each dorm supervisor had the power to deny admittance based upon his judgment alone, so how well this very important rule was enforced depended on who the supervisor was for the night. Some were better than others at spotting who was "under the influence", and this ability included realizing how some people were more skillful at hiding their intoxication than others. Borderline individuals could be admitted one night, then denied entry the next by another supervisor. Helpful Harry was usually in this category. In fact I remember once when he was allowed in at first, then kicked out a short time later, not because he had shown any overt signs of intoxication, but simply because the supervisor changed his mind. So this rule was not always uniformly enforced, although a reasonable effort was made to do so. Surly Kid's untimely exit happened only once.

SIGN-IN ENDS AT 10 PM SHARP. ARRANGEMENTS FOR LATE ARRIVAL MUST BE MADE IN ADVANCE AND WILL ONLY BE MADE TO ACCOMMODATE WORK OR MEDICAL SITUATIONS.

This rule was strictly enforced, although there were a few residents who had night jobs and were allowed to arrive later than 10PM.

There was another aspect to signing-in that was never explicitly stated in writing but was important nevertheless; that is, each person's sign-in remained valid only as long as he stayed in the shelter or within the immediate vicinity of it until the dorm was closed for the night at 10:15 PM. The immediate vicinity included the parking lot and driveway. Once someone who had signed-in went beyond the end of the driveway onto New Street, he instantly nullified his sign-in and could no longer stay the night. On its face this seemed to be an easy enough rule to obey-- once you sign-in, don't go wandering off somewhere. But Surly Kid and a few others seemed to have a problem with it, especially during the warmer weather when the dorm would sometimes open earlier than usual. Ornery One soon realized this, and would station himself on the shelter's front porch which commanded a good view of the entire driveway. He would then snitch on anyone who ventured out too far after signing-in.

LAST CIGARETTE IS AT 10:15 PM; NO SMOKING IN THE BUILDING OR IN THE FRONT ENTRANCE OF THE BUILDING. YOU MAY NOT LEAVE THE BUILDING AFTER 10:15 PM. IF YOU DO, YOU WILL NOT BE ALLOWED TO REENTER. LIGHTS OUT OCCURS PRECISELY AT 10:30 PM. AT THIS TIME YOU ARE TO BE SHOWERED AND IN BED. NO LAUNDRY, TV OR ANY OTHER ACTIVITIES SHOULD CONTINUE AFTER 10:30 PM.

The rule against smoking in the building was strictly observed, and I don't remember anyone ever breaking it. For those who smoked a lot, like Bullpen Coach and Marlboro Man, the last 30-45 minutes before 10:15 PM were vital-- it was their last chance to have a cigarette for the night and they, along with several others, took full advantage of it, which is why there were so few people using the bathroom during the same period.

At 10:15 PM the outside door was shut and nobody was supposed to leave until the next morning. This rule was generally observed because anyone who was still in the dorm by then usually wanted to stay for the night. But occasionally The Blustery Gent would get restless and leave in the middle of the night. He simply pushed the door open and went out, and when it closed behind him it locked automatically. His unexpected departures would affect the chore schedule for the morning, so efforts were made to dissuade him from doing this.

The lights out rule was strictly observed, but there were a few times when certain people would continue to use their laptop computers in the dark.

YOU MAY STORE YOUR PERSONAL BELONGINGS IN A LOCKER. YOU MUST PROVIDE YOUR OWN LOCK. DO NOT LEAVE PERSONAL BELONGINGS LYING AROUND THE FACILITY OR AROUND YOUR COT. REMEMBER THAT ON THE FIRST OF EVERY MONTH LOCKERS ARE CLEANED OUT. IF YOU DO NOT CLEAN OUT YOUR ITEMS, THEY WILL BE DISPOSED OF.

This regulation highlights one of the advantages that the city shelter had over some of the privately-run ones which did not offer any lockable storage space for personal belongings. I never kept more than a few basic items in my locker since it had to be cleaned out periodically. The rule about keeping all your stuff in your locker was not strictly enforced because some people, like Feisty Kid and The Blustery Gent, always showed up carrying huge backpacks that they were allowed to keep near their cots.